SAINT PATRICK

EDITED AND PRESENTED BY IAIN MACDONALD

FLORIS BOOKS

First published in 1992 by Floris Books

© Floris Books, Edinburgh, 1992

British Library CIP Data available

ISBN 0-86315-144-2

Printed in Great Britain
by Courier International, East Kilbride

Contents

Introduction   7

The Letter to the soldiers of Coroticus   11

The Confession of St Patrick   23

The Lorica (Patrick's Breast-plate)   55

Introduction

St Patrick was born in an unknown part of Britain, probably in the south west, around the year 385 ad. His full name was Magonus Sucatus Patricius. Born into a family of some means and social standing, Patrick led a fairly undisciplined youth, according to his own account. Although his father was a deacon, there does not appear to have been a strong religious influence in the family home.

At the age of sixteen, Patrick was captured by Irish raiders and sold as a slave in Ireland. He spent the next six years as a shepherd in the service of his master, who — tradition has it — was a druid. Then he heard a voice in his dreams telling him to go home. He walked two hundred miles to find the ship that his dream told him would be waiting for him. He was taken on a boat carrying Irish hounds to Gaul.

It is not clear when Patrick finally reached his home in Britain again. During this period, he repeatedly heard the voice of the Irish calling him back and he underwent profound spiritual experiences. He decided to seek holy orders and went to Gaul for his studies.

In 429 the question arose of sending the Irish a

bishop of their own. Patrick's name was turned down, apparently after indiscretions of his youth were revealed to the synod, and Palladius was sent instead. But in 432 Patrick followed, only to find on his arrival in Ireland that Palladius was dead. Returning to Gaul, Patrick was now consecrated bishop of Ireland and set off to take up his new responsibilities later in the same year.

Once in Ireland, Patrick set about converting the princes of the many small states into which the country was divided. He recruited many of his new clergy from the ranks of the young nobility. He also spread the virtues of the monastic life for which he had great affection. Patrick's own episcopal see he founded at Armagh.

His task of converting all of Ireland was fraught with difficulty, as there was opposition not only from the old druidic tradition, but also from some elements of the ruling classes. But within the space of thirty years, the country was almost entirely Christian. This astonishing missionary work was given the official seal of approval by Pope Leo I and, according to tradition, Patrick died on March 17, 461, in Ulster.

Patrick's writings

Little remains of Patrick's own writings: two letters, some fragments, a set of religious rules or canons, and the so-called Lorica, *or breast-plate. They are among the oldest surviving documents of the Irish church.*

The three documents included here are: the letter to the soldiers of Coroticus, the open letter known as the Confession, *written towards the end of Patrick's life, and the* Lorica. *They give evidence in very different ways of the strong and inspirational personality that Patrick must have been for his contemporaries.*

Of these, the authenticity of the two letters is not seriously questioned by most modern scholars. The Lorica, *perhaps the most famous of all the documents associated with Patrick, was put in writing only about the ninth century but clearly had been passed down orally from about the sixth century. Its authorship is by no means certain but has long been linked with the name of Patrick. Whoever the original author of the* Lorica, *the splendour of its poetry and the depth of its spiritual inspiration have never been in doubt.*

The letter to Coroticus

Coroticus was a fifth-century British prince, possibly to be identified with the Welsh prince, Ceredig, founder of the principality of Cardigan. He was one of a number of local rulers who had filled the power vacuum since the withdrawal of the Romans in 407. As a Christian, he became a defender of the Roman Christians in south-west Britain against pirates and raiders of the very type that had abducted Patrick in his youth.

It seems that Coroticus had become so powerful that he was able to launch reprisal raids against Ireland itself. On one of these raids, his men attacked and slaughtered a number of Patrick's new converts and abducted the rest of the community into slavery.

Patrick's clerics delivered a letter of protest, only to be met with scorn. In this forceful and furious letter to Coroticus' soldiers, Patrick now demands retribution and the excommunication of the guilty, even of Coroticus himself.

The letter has many similarities of style and form with the later Confession and throws much light on the strained relations that Patrick had with the

Christians of Britain who opposed his episcopacy. Quoting that "a prophet hath no honour in his own country," Patrick expresses with powerful emotions not only his own sense of rejection by the British people, but also the strength of his attachment to his adopted people of Ireland.

The translation here is that of Ludwig Bieler, first published in 1953, based on his own revised edition of 1950.

Patrick, a sinner, unlearned, resident in Ireland, declare myself to be a bishop. Most assuredly I believe that what I am I have received from God. And so I live among barbarians, a stranger and exile for the love of God. He is witness that this is so. Not that I wished my mouth to utter anything so hard and harsh; but I am forced by the zeal of God; and the truth of Christ has wrung it from me, out of love for my neighbours and sons for whom I gave up my country and parents and my life to the point of death. If I be worthy, I live for my God to teach the heathen, even though some may despise me.

With my own hand I have written and composed these words, to be given, delivered, and sent to the soldiers of Coroticus; I do not say, to my fellow citizens, or to fellow citizens of the holy Romans, but to fellow citizens of the demons, because of their evil works. Like our enemies, they live in death, allies of the Scots and the apostate Picts. Dripping with blood, they welter in the blood of innocent Christians, whom I have begotten into the number for God and confirmed in Christ!

The day after the newly baptized, anointed with chrism, in white garments had been slain — the fragrance was still on their foreheads when they were butchered and slaughtered with the sword by the above-mentioned people — I sent a letter with a holy presbyter whom I had taught from his childhood, clerics accompanying him, asking them to return to us some of the booty and the baptized they had made captives. They only jeered at them.

Hence I do not know what to lament more: those who have been slain, or those whom they have taken captive, or those whom the devil has ensnared. Together with him they will be slaves in Hell in an eternal punishment; for who commits sin is a slave and will be called a son of the devil.

Wherefore let every God-fearing man know that they are enemies of me and of Christ my God, for whom I am an ambassador. Parricide! fratricide! ravening wolves that eat the people of the Lord as they eat bread! As is said, *The wicked, O Lord, have destroyed Thy law,* which but recently He had excellently and kindly planted in Ireland, and which had established itself by the grace of God.

I make no false claim. I share in the work of those whom He called and predestined to preach the Gospel amidst grave persecutions unto the end of the earth, even if the enemy shows his jealousy through the tyranny of Coroticus, a man who has no respect for God nor for His priests whom He chose, giving them the highest, divine, and sublime power, that whom they should bind upon earth should be bound also in heaven.

Wherefore, then I plead with you earnestly, ye holy and humble of heart, it is not permissible to court the favour of such people, nor to

take food or drink with them, nor even to accept
their alms, until they make reparation to God in
hardships, through penance, with shedding of
tears, and set free the baptized servants of God
and handmaids of Christ, for whom He died and
was crucified.

*The most High disapproveth the gifts of the
wicked. ... He that offereth sacrifice of the goods of the
poor, is as one that sacrificeth the son in the presence
of his father. The riches,* it is written, *which he has
gathered unjustly, shall be vomited up from his belly;
the angel of death drags him away, by the fury of
dragons he shall be tormented, the viper's tongue shall
kill him, unquenchable fire devoureth him.* And so
— *Woe to those who fill themselves with what is not
their own;* or, *What doth it profit a man that he gain
the whole world, and suffer the loss of his own soul.*

It would be too tedious to discuss and set
forth everything in detail, to gather from the
whole Law testimonies against such greed.
Avarice is a deadly sin. *Though shalt not covet thy
neighbour's goods. Thou shalt not kill.* A murderer
cannot be with Christ. Whosoever hates his
brother is accounted a murderer. Or, *He that
loveth not his brother abideth in death.* How much

more guilty is he that has stained his hands with
the blood of the sons of God whom He has of
late purchased in the utmost part of the earth
through the call of our littleness!

Did I come to Ireland without God, through
the call of the flesh? Who compelled me?
Because I am bound by the Spirit, never to see
any of my own kinsfolk. Is it of my own doing
that I have holy mercy on the people who once
took me captive and made away with the
servants and maids of my father's house? I was
freeborn. I am the son of a decurion. But I sold
my noble rank — I am neither ashamed nor
sorry — for the good of others. Thus I am a
servant in Christ to a foreign nation for the
unspeakable glory of life everlasting which is in
Christ Jesus our Lord.

And if my own people do not know me, *a
prophet hath no honour in his own country*. Perhaps
we are not of the same fold and have not one and
the same God as father, as is written: *He that is
not with me, is against me, and he that gathereth not
with me scattereth*. It is not right that one
destroys, another builds up. I seek not the things
that are mine.

It is not my grace, but God who has given this solicitude into my heart, to be one of His hunters or fishers whom God once foretold would come in the last days.

I am hated. What shall I do, Lord? I am most despised. Look, Thy sheep around me are torn to pieces and driven away, and that by those robbers, by the orders of the hostile-minded Coroticus. Far from the love of God is a man who hands over Christians to the Picts and Scots. Ravening wolves have devoured the flock of the Lord, which in Ireland was indeed growing splendidly with the greatest care; and the sons and daughters of kings were monks and virgins of Christ — I cannot count their number. Wherefore, be not pleased with the wrong done to the just; even to hell it shall not please.

Who of the saints would not shudder to be merry with such persons or to enjoy a meal with them. They have filled their houses with the spoils of dead Christians, they live on plunder. They do not know, the wretches, that what they offer their friends and sons as food is deadly poison, just as Eve did not understand that it was death she gave to her husband. So are all that do evil: they work death as their eternal punishment.

This is the custom of the Roman Christians of Gaul: they send holy and able men to the Franks and other heathen with so many thousand *solidi* to ransom baptized captives. You prefer to kill and sell them to a foreign nation that has no knowledge of God. You betray the members of Christ as it were into a brothel. What hope have you in God, or anyone who thinks as you do, or converses with you in words of flattery? God will judge. For Scripture says: *Not only they that do evil are worthy to be condemned, but they also that consent to them.*

I do not know what I should say further about the departed ones of the sons of God, whom the sword has touched all too harshly. For Scripture says: *Weep with them that weep;* and again: *If one member be grieved, let all members grieve with it.* Hence the Church mourns and laments her sons and daughters whom the sword has not yet slain, but who were removed and carried off to faraway lands, where sin abounds openly, grossly, impudently. There people who were freeborn have been sold, Christians made slaves, and that, too, in the service of the abominable, wicked, and apostate Picts!

Therefore I shall raise my voice in sadness and grief: O you fair and beloved brethren and sons whom I have begotten in Christ, countless of number, what can I do for you? I am not worthy to come to the help of God or men. The wickedness of the wicked hath prevailed over us. We have been made, as it were, strangers. Perhaps they do not believe that we have received one and the same baptism, or have one and the same God as father. For them it is a disgrace that we are Irish. *Have ye not,* as is written, *one God. Have ye, every one of you, forsaken his neighbour?*

Therefore I grieve for you, I grieve, my dearly beloved. But again, I rejoice within myself. I have not laboured for nothing, and my journeying abroad has not been in vain. And if this horrible, unspeakable crime did happen — thanks be to God, you have left the world and have gone to Paradise as baptized faithful. I see you: you have begun to journey where night shall be no more, nor mourning, nor death; but you shall leap like calves loosened from their bonds, and you shall tread down the wicked, and they shall be ashes under your feet.

You, then, will reign with the apostles, and prophets, and martyrs. You will take possession of eternal kingdoms, as He Himself testifies, saying: *They shall come from the east and from the west, and shall sit down with Abraham, and Isaac, and Jacob in the kingdom of heaven. Without are dogs, and sorcerers, ... and murderers;* and liars and perjurers have their portion in the pool of everlasting fire. Not without reason does the Apostle say: *Where the just man shall scarcely be saved, where shall the sinner and ungodly transgressor of the law find himself?*

Where, then, will Coroticus with his criminals, rebels against Christ, where will they see themselves, they who distribute baptized women as prizes — for a miserable temporal kingdom, which will pass away in a moment? As a cloud or smoke that is dispersed by the wind, so shall the deceitful wicked perish at the presence of the Lord; but the just shall feast with great constancy with Christ; they shall judge nations, and rule over wicked kings for ever and ever. Amen.

I testify before God and His angels that it will be so as He indicated to my ignorance. It is not my words that I have set forth in Latin, but those of God and the apostles and prophets, who have never lied. He that believes shall be saved: but he that believes not shall be condemned, God has spoken.

I ask earnestly that whoever is a willing servant of God be a carrier of this letter, so that on no account it be suppressed or hidden by anyone, but rather be read before all the people, and in the presence of Coroticus himself. May God inspire them sometime to recover their senses for God, repenting, however late, their heinous deeds — murderers of the brethren of the Lord! — and to set free the baptized women whom they took captive, in order that they may deserve to live to God, and be made whole, here and in eternity! Be peace to the Father, and to the Son, and to the Holy Spirit. Amen.

The confession

The Confession of St Patrick was written as an open letter, thanking God for his guidance and grace, justifying his rule as bishop, and confessing his own human weaknesses. There are similarities to St Augustine's Confessions and to St Paul's Letter to the Corinthians.

The Confession is our main source of information about Patrick's own life, though its approach to historical narrative is rather wayward. The letter was certainly not written as an autobiography, more as a kind of apologia and spiritual bequest to his church in Ireland. It is not surprising then, if still annoying for historians, to find important facts and details missing. To fill the gaps, we have to look at other Irish documents and at traditions recorded elsewhere.

Added to this, Patrick himself admits that he is not skilled as a writer. Tradition has him as a man of action rather than of great education and learning. His writing frequently rambles around his theme and is fairly disordered in its chronology.

The great quality of Patrick's Confession is the strength and energy of personality shining through.

The fervour and conviction of his mission to Ireland, the powerful influence of his spiritual experiences, and his fearless confrontation with his enemies — all of these betray a truly exceptional personality, guided by some inner strength towards a far from ordinary destiny.

The present text is the translation made by Ludwig Bieler, first published in 1953 and based on his own revised edition of the Latin text. The interpretation of a number of passages is still subject to question and most scholarly editions are accompanied by copious notes.

am Patrick, a sinner, most unlearned, the least of all the faithful, and utterly despised by many. My father was Calpornius, a deacon, son of Potitus, a priest, of the village Bannavem Taburniae; he had a country seat nearby, and there I was taken captive.

I was then about sixteen years of age. I did not know the true God. I was taken into captivity to Ireland with many thousands of people — and deservedly so, because we turned away from God, and did not keep His commandments, and did not obey our priests, who used to remind us of our salvation. And the Lord *brought over us the wrath of His anger and scattered us among many nations,* even unto the utmost part of the earth, where now my littleness is placed among strangers.

And there *the Lord opened the sense of my unbelief* that I might at last remember my sins and *be converted with all my heart to the Lord my God,* who had regard for my abjection, and mercy on my youth and ignorance, and watched over me before I knew Him, and before I was able to distinguish between good and evil, and guarded me, and comforted me as would a father his son.

Hence I cannot be silent — nor, indeed, is it expedient — about the great benefits and the great grace which the Lord has deigned to bestow upon me in the land of my captivity; for this we can give to God in return after having been chastened by Him, to exalt and praise His wonders before every nation that is anywhere under the heaven.

Because there is no other God, nor ever was, nor will be, than God the Father unbegotten, without beginning, from whom is all beginning, the Lord of the universe, as we have been taught; and His son Jesus Christ, whom we declare to have always been with the Father, spiritually and ineffably begotten by the Father before the beginning of the world, before all beginning; and by Him are made all things visible and invisible. He was made man, and, having defeated death, was received into heaven by the Father; *and He hath given Him all power over all names in heaven, on earth, and under the earth, and every tongue shall confess to Him that Jesus Christ is Lord and God*, in whom we believe, and whose advent we expect soon to be, judge of the living and of the dead, who will render to every man according to his deeds; and *He has poured forth upon us abundantly the Holy Spirit*, the gift and pledge of immortality, who makes those who believe and obey sons of God and joint heirs with Christ; and Him do we confess and adore, one God in the Trinity of the Holy Name.

For He Himself has said through the Prophet:

Call upon me in the day of thy trouble, and I will deliver thee, and thou shalt glorify me. And again He says: *It is honourable to reveal and confess the works of God.*

Although I am imperfect in many things, I nevertheless wish that my brethren and kinsmen should know what sort of person I am, so that they may understand my heart's desire.

I know well the testimony of my Lord, who in the Psalm declares: *Thou wilt destroy them that speak a lie.* And again He says: *The mouth that belieth killeth the soul.* And the same Lord says in the Gospel: *Every idle word that men shall speak, they shall render an account for it on the day of judgment.*

And so I should dread exceedingly, with fear and trembling, this sentence on that day when no one will be able to escape or hide, but we all, without exception, shall have to give an account even of our smallest sins before the judgment seat of the Lord Christ.

For this reason I long had in mind to write, but hesitated until now; I was afraid of exposing myself to the talk of men, because I have not studied like the others, who thoroughly imbibed law and Sacred Scripture, and never had to change from the language of their childhood days, but were able to make it still more perfect. In our case, what I had to say had to be translated into a tongue foreign to me, as can be easily proved from the savour of my writing, which betrays how little instruction and training I have had in the art of words; for, so says Scripture, *by the tongue will be discovered the wise man, and understanding, and knowledge, and the teaching of truth.*

But of what help is an excuse, however true, especially if combined with presumption, since now, in my old age, I strive for something that I did not acquire in youth? It was my sins that prevented me from fixing in my mind what before I had barely read through. But who believes me, though I should repeat what I started out with?

As a youth, nay, almost as a boy not able to speak, I was taken captive, before I knew what to pursue and what to avoid. Hence today I blush and fear exceedingly to reveal my lack of education; for I am unable to tell my story to those versed in the art of concise writing — in such a way, I mean, as my spirit and mind long to do, and so that the sense of my words expresses what I feel.

But if indeed it had been given to me as it was given to others, then I would not be silent because of my desire of thanksgiving; and if perhaps some people think me arrogant for doing so in spite of my lack of knowledge and my slow tongue, it is, after all, written: *The stammering tongues shall quickly learn to speak peace.*

How much more should we earnestly strive to do this, we, who are, so Scripture says, *a letter of Christ for salvation unto the utmost part of the earth,* and, though not an eloquent one, yet ... *written in your hearts, not with ink, but with the spirit of the living God!* And again the Spirit witnesses that even rusticity was created by the Highest.

Whence I, once rustic, exiled, unlearned, who does not know how to provide for the future, this at least I know most certainly that before I was humiliated I was like a stone lying in the deep mire; and He that is mighty came and in His mercy lifted me up, and raised me aloft, and placed me on the top of the wall. And therefore I ought to cry out aloud and so also render something to the Lord for His great benefits here and in eternity — benefits which the mind of men is unable to appraise.

Wherefore, then, be astonished, ye great and little that fear God, and you men of letters on your estates, listen and pore over this. Who was it that roused up me, the fool that I am, from the midst of those who in the eyes of men are wise, and expert in law, and powerful in word and in everything? And He inspired me — me, the outcast of this world — before others, to be the man (if only I could!) who, with fear and reverence and without blame, should faithfully serve the people to whom the love of Christ conveyed and gave me for the duration of my life, if I should be worthy; yes indeed, to serve them humbly and sincerely.

In the light, therefore, of our faith in the Trinity I must make this choice, regardless of danger I must make known the gift of God and everlasting consolation, without fear and frankly I must spread everywhere the name of God so that after my decease I may leave a bequest to my brethren and sons whom I have baptized in the Lord — so many thousands of people.

And I was not worthy, nor was I such that the Lord should grant this to His servant; that after my misfortunes and so great difficulties, after my captivity, after the lapse of so many years, He should give me so great a grace in behalf of that nation — a thing which once, in my youth, I never expected nor thought of.

ut after I came to Ireland — every day I had to tend sheep, and many times a day I prayed — the love of God and His fear came to me more and more, and my faith was strengthened. And my spirit was moved so that in a single day I would say as many as a hundred prayers, and almost as many in the night, and this even when I was staying in the woods and on the mountain; and I used to get up for prayer before daylight, through snow, through frost, through rain, and I felt no harm, and there was no sloth in me — as I now see, because the spirit within me was then fervent.

And there one night I heard in my sleep a
voice saying to me: "It is well that you fast, soon
you will go to your own country." And again,
after a short while, I heard a voice saying to me:
"See, your ship is ready." And it was not near,
but at a distance of perhaps two hundred miles,
and I had never been there, nor did I know a
living soul there; and then I took to flight, and I
left the man with whom I had stayed for six
years. And I went in the strength of God who
directed my way to my good, and I feared
nothing until I came to that ship.

And the day that I arrived the ship was set
afloat, and I said that I was able to pay for my
passage with them. But the captain was not
pleased, and with indignation he answered
harshly: "It is of no use for you to ask us to go
along with us." And when I heard this, I left
them in order to return to the hut where I was
staying. And as I went, I began to pray; and
before I had ended my prayer, I heard one of
them shouting behind me: "Come, hurry, we
shall take you on in good faith; make friends
with us in whatever way you like." And so on
that day I refused to seek their protection for fear

of God, but rather hoped they would come to the faith of Jesus Christ, because they were pagans. And thus I had my way with them, and we set sail at once.

And after three days we reached land, and for twenty-eight days we travelled through deserted country. And they lacked food, and hunger overcame them; and the next day the captain said to me: "Tell me, Christian: you say that your God is great and all-powerful; why, then, do you not pray for us? As you can see, we are suffering from hunger; it is unlikely indeed that we shall ever see a human being again."

I said to them full of confidence: "Be truly converted with all your heart to the Lord my God, because nothing is impossible for Him, that this day He may send you food on your way until you be satisfied; for He has abundance everywhere." And, with the help of God, so it came to pass: suddenly a herd of pigs appeared on the road before our eyes, and they killed many of them; and there they stopped for two nights and fully recovered their strength, and their hounds received their fill, for many of them had grown weak and were half-dead along the way. And from that day they had plenty of food. They also found wild honey, and offered some of it to me, and one of them said: "This we offer in sacrifice." Thanks be to God, I tasted none of it.

That same night, when I was asleep, Satan assailed me violently, a thing I shall remember as long as I shall be in this body. And he fell upon me like a huge rock, and I could not stir a limb. But whence came it into my mind, ignorant as I am, to call upon Elias? And meanwhile I saw the sun rise in the sky, and while I was shouting "Elias! Elias!" with all my might, suddenly the splendour of that sun fell on me and immediately freed me of all misery. And I believe that I was sustained by Christ my Lord, and that His Spirit was even then crying out in my behalf, and I hope it will be so on the day of my tribulation, as is written in the Gospel: *On that day*, the Lord declares, *it is not you that speak, but the Spirit of your Father that speaketh in you.*

And once again, after many years, I fell into captivity. On that first night I stayed with them.

I heard a divine message saying to me: "Two months will you be with them." And so it came to pass: on the sixtieth night thereafter the Lord delivered me out of their hands.

Also on our way God gave us food and fire and dry weather every day, until, on the tenth day, we met people. As I said above, we travelled twenty-eight days through deserted country, and the night that we met people we had no food left.

And again after a few years I was in Britain with my people, who received me as their son, and sincerely besought me that now at last, having suffered so many hardships, I should not leave them and go elsewhere.

And there I saw in the night the vision of a man, whose name was Victoricus, coming as it were from Ireland, with countless letters. And he gave me one of them, and I read the opening words of the letter, which were: "The voice of the Irish"; and as I read the beginning of the letter I thought that at the same moment I heard their voice — they were those beside the Wood of Voclut, which is near the Western Sea — and thus did they cry out as with one mouth: "We ask thee, boy, come and walk among us once more."

And I was quite broken in heart, and could read no further, and so I woke up. Thanks be to God, after many years the Lord gave to them according to their cry.

And another night — whether within me, or beside me, I know not, God knoweth — they called me most unmistakably with words which I heard but could not understand, except that at the end of the prayer He spoke thus: "He that has laid down His life for thee, it is He that speaketh in thee"; and so I awoke full of joy.

And again I saw Him praying in me, and I was as it were within my body, and I heard Him above me, that is, over the inward man, and there He prayed mightily with groanings. And all the time I was astonished, and wondered, and thought with myself who it could be that prayed in me. But at the end of the prayer He spoke, saying that He was the Spirit; and so I woke up, and remembered the Apostle saying: *The Spirit helpeth the infirmities of our prayer. For we know not what we should pray for as we ought; but the Spirit Himself asketh for us with unspeakable groanings, which cannot be expressed in words*; and again: *The Lord our advocate asketh for us.*

And when I was attacked by a number of my seniors who came forth and brought up my sins against my laborious episcopate, on that day indeed was I struck so that I might have fallen now and for eternity; but the Lord graciously spared the stranger and sojourner for His name and came mightily to my help in this affliction. Verily, not slight was the shame and blame that fell upon me! I ask God that it may not be reckoned to them as sin.

As cause for proceeding against me they found — after thirty years! — a confession I had made before I was a deacon. In the anxiety of my troubled mind I confided to my dearest friend what I had done in my boyhood one day, nay, in one hour, because I was not yet strong. I know not, God knoweth — whether I was then fifteen years old; and I did not believe in the living God, nor did I so from my childhood, but lived in death and unbelief until I was severely chastised and really humiliated, by hunger and nakedness, and that daily.

On the other hand, I did not go to Ireland of

my own accord, not until I had nearly perished; but this was rather for my good, for thus was I purged by the Lord; and He made me fit so that I might be now what was once far from me — that I should care and labour for the salvation of others, whereas then I did not even care about myself.

On that day, then, when I was rejected by those referred to and mentioned above, in that night I saw a vision of the night. There was a writing without honour against my face, and at the same time I heard God's voice saying to me: "We have seen with displeasure the face of Deisignatus" (thus revealing his name). He did not say: "Thou hast seen," but: "We have seen," as if He included Himself, as He says: *He who toucheth you toucheth as it were the apple of my eye.*

Therefore I give Him thanks who hath strengthened me in everything, as He did not frustrate the journey upon which I had decided, and the work which I had learned from Christ my Lord; but I rather felt after this no little strength, and my trust was proved right before God and men.

And so I say boldly, my conscience does not

blame me now or in the future: God is my witness that I have not lied in the account which I have given you.

But the more am I sorry for my dearest friend that we had to hear what he said. To him I had confided my very soul! And I was told by some of the brethren before that defence — at which I was not present, nor was I in Britain, nor was it suggested by me — that he would stand up for me in my absence.

He had even said to me in person: "Look, you should be raised to the rank of bishop!" — of which I was not worthy. But whence did it come to him afterwards that he let me down before all, good and evil, and publicly, in a matter in which he had favoured me before spontaneously and gladly — and not he alone, but the Lord, who is greater than all?

Enough of this. I must not, however, hide God's gift which He bestowed upon me in the land of my captivity; because then I earnestly sought Him, and there I found Him, and He saved me from all evil because — so I believe — of His Spirit that dwelleth in me. Again, boldly said. But God knows it, had this been said to me?

by a man, I had perhaps remained silent for the love of Christ.

Hence, then, I give unwearied thanks to God, who kept me faithful in the day of my temptation, so that today I can confidently offer Him my soul as a living sacrifice — to Christ my Lord, who saved me out of all my troubles. Thus I can say: "Who am I, O Lord, and to what hast Thou called me, Thou who didst assist me with such divine power that today I constantly exalt and magnify Thy name among the heathens wherever I may be, and not only in good days but also in tribulations?

So indeed I must accept with equanimity whatever befalls me, be it good or evil, and always give thanks to God, who taught me to trust in Him always without hesitation, and who must have heard my prayer so that I, however ignorant I was, in the last days I dared to undertake such a holy and wonderful work — thus imitating somehow those who, as the Lord once foretold, would preach His Gospel for a testimony to all nations before the end of the world. So we have seen it, and so it has been fulfilled: indeed, we are witnesses that the

Gospel has been preached unto those parts beyond which there lives nobody.

ow, it would be tedious to give a detailed account of all my labours or even a part of them. Let me tell you briefly how the merciful God often freed me from slavery and from twelve dangers in which my life was at stake — not to mention numerous plots, which I cannot express in words; for I do not want to bore my readers. But God is my witness, who knows all things even before they come to pass, as He used to forewarn even me, poor wretch that I am, of many things by a divine message.

How came I by this wisdom, which was not in me, who neither knew the number of my days nor knew what God was? Whence was given to me afterwards the gift so great, so salutary — to know God and to love Him, although at the price of leaving my country and my parents?

And many gifts were offered to me in sorrow

and tears, and I offended the donors, much against the wishes of some of my seniors; but, guided by God, in no way did I agree with them or acquiesce. It was not grace of my own, but God, who is strong in me and resists them all — as He had done when I came to the people of Ireland to preach the Gospel, and to suffer insult from the unbelievers, hearing the reproach of my going abroad, and many persecutions even unto bonds, and to give my free birth for the benefit of others; and, should I be worthy, I am prepared to give even my life without hesitation and most gladly for His name, and it is there that I wish to spend it until I die, if the Lord would grant it to me.

For I am very much God's debtor, who gave me such great grace that many people were reborn in God through me and afterwards confirmed, and that clerics were ordained for them everywhere, for a people just coming to the faith, whom the Lord took from the utmost parts of the earth, as He once had promised through His prophets: *To Thee the Gentiles shall come from the ends of the earth and shall say: "How false are the idols that our fathers got for themselves, and there is no profit in them"*; and again: *I have set Thee as a light among the Gentiles, that Thou mayest be for salvation unto the utmost part of the earth.*

And there I wish to wait for His promise who surely never deceives, as He promises in the Gospel: *They shall come from the east and the west, and shall sit down with Abraham and Isaac and Jacob* — as we believe the faithful will come from all the world.

For that reason, therefore, we ought to fish well and diligently, as the Lord exhorts in advance and teaches, saying: *Come ye after me, and I will make you to be fishers of men.* And again He says through the prophets: *Behold, I send many fishers and hunters, saith God,* and so on. Hence it was most necessary to spread our nets so that a great multitude and throng might be caught for God, and that there be clerics everywhere to baptize and exhort a people in need and want, as the Lord in the Gospel states, exhorts, and teaches, saying: *Going therefore now, teach ye all nations, baptizing them in the name of the Father, and the Son, and the Holy Spirit, teaching them to observe all things whatsoever I have commanded you: and behold I am with you all days even to the consummation of the world.* And again He says: *Go ye therefore into the whole world, and preach the Gospel to every creature. He that believeth and is baptized shall be saved; but he that believeth not shall be condemned.* And again: *This Gospel of the kingdom shall be preached in the whole world for a testimony to all nations, and then shall come the end.*

And so too the Lord announces through the prophet, and says: *And it shall come to pass, in the last days, saith the Lord, I will pour out of my Spirit upon all flesh; and your sons and your daughters shall prophesy, and your young men shall see visions, and your old men shall dream dreams. And upon my servants indeed, and upon my handmaids will I pour out in those days of my Spirit, and they shall prophesy.*

And in Osee He says: *"I will call that which was not my people, my people; ... and her that had not obtained mercy, one that hath obtained mercy. And it shall be in the place where it was said: You are not my people. There they shall be called the sons of the living God."*

Hence, how did it come to pass in Ireland that those who never had a knowledge of God, but until now always worshipped idols and things impure, have now been made a people of the Lord, and are called sons of God, that the sons and daughters of the kings of the Irish are seen to be monks and virgins of Christ?

Among others, a blessed Irishwoman of noble birth, beautiful, full-grown, whom I had baptized, came to us after some days for a particular reason: she told us that she had received a message from a messenger of God, and he admonished her to be a virgin of Christ and draw near to God. Thanks be to God, on the sixth day after this she most laudably and eagerly chose what all virgins of Christ do. Not that their fathers agree with them; no — they often even suffer persecution and undeserved reproaches from their parents; and yet their number is ever increasing. How many have been reborn there so as to be of our kind, I do not know — not to mention widows and those who practice continence.

But greatest is the suffering of those women who live in slavery. All the time they have to endure terror and threats. But the Lord gave His grace to many of His maidens; for, though they are forbidden to do so, they follow Him bravely.

Wherefore, then, even if I wished to leave them and go to Britain — and how I would have loved to go to my country and my parents, and also to Gaul in order to visit the brethren and to see the face of the saints of my Lord! God knows it that I much desired it; but I am bound by the Spirit, who gives evidence against me if I do this, telling me that I shall be guilty; and I am afraid of losing the labour which I have begun — nay, not I, but Christ the Lord who bade me come here and stay with them for the rest of my life, if the Lord will, and will guard me from every evil way that I may not sin before Him.

This, I presume, I ought to do, but I do not trust myself as long as I am in this body of death, for strong is he who daily strives to turn me away from the faith and the purity of true religion to which I have devoted myself to the end of my life to Christ my Lord. But the hostile flesh is ever dragging us unto death, that is, towards the forbidden satisfaction of one's desires; and I know that in part I did not lead a perfect life as did the other faithful; but I acknowledge it to my Lord, and do not blush before Him, because I lie not: from the time I came to know Him in my youth, the love of God and the fear of Him have grown in me, and up to now, thanks to the grace of God, I have kept the faith.

And let those who will, laugh and scorn — I shall not be silent; nor shall I hide the signs and wonders which the Lord has shown me many years before they came to pass, as He knows everything even before the times of the world.

Hence I ought unceasingly to give thanks to God who often pardoned my folly and my carelessness, and on more than one occasion spared His great wrath on me, who was chosen to be His helper and who was slow to do as was shown me and as the Spirit suggested. And the Lord had mercy on me thousands and thousands of times because He saw that I was ready, but that I did not know what to do in the circumstances. For many tried to prevent this my mission; they would even talk to each other behind my back and say: "Why does this fellow throw himself into danger among enemies who have no knowledge of God?" It was not malice, but it did not appeal to them because — and to this I own myself — of my rusticity. And I did not realize at once the grace that was then in me; now I understand that I should have done so before.

Now I have given a simple account to my brethren and fellow servants who have believed me because of what I said and still say in order to strengthen and confirm your faith. Would that you, too, would strive for greater things and do better! This will be my glory, for a wise son is the glory of his father.

You know, and so does God, how I have lived among you from my youth in the true faith and in sincerity of heart. Likewise, as regards the heathen among whom I live, I have been faithful to them, and so I shall be. God knows it, I have overreached none of them, nor would I think of doing so, for the sake of God and His Church, for fear of raising persecution against them and all of us, and for fear that through me the name of the Lord be blasphemed; for it is written: *Woe to the man through whom the name of the Lord is blasphemed.*

For although I be rude in all things, nevertheless I have tried somehow to keep myself safe, and that, too, for my Christian brethren, and the virgins of Christ, and the pious women who of their own accord made me gifts and laid on the altar some of their ornaments; and I gave them back to them, and they were offended that I did so. But I did it for the hope of lasting success — in order to preserve myself cautiously in everything so that they might not seize upon me or the ministry of my service, under the pretext of dishonesty, and that I would not even in the smallest matter give the infidels an opportunity to defame or defile.

When I baptized so many thousands of people, did I perhaps expect from any of them as much as half a screpall? Tell me, and I will restore it to you. Or when the Lord ordained clerics everywhere through my unworthy person and I conferred the ministry upon them free, if I asked any of them as much as the price of my shoes, speak against me and I will return it to you.

On the contrary, I spent money for you that they might receive me; and I went to you and everywhere for your sake in many dangers, even to the farthest districts, beyond which there lived nobody and where nobody had ever come to baptize, or to ordain clergy, or to confirm the people. With the grace of the Lord, I did everything lovingly and gladly for your salvation.

All the while I used to give presents to the kings, besides the fees I paid to their sons who travel with me. Even so they laid hands on me and my companions, and on that day they eagerly wished to kill me; but my time had not yet come. And everything they found with us they took away, and me they put in irons; and on the fourteenth day the Lord delivered me from their power, and our belongings were returned to us because of God and our dear friends whom we had seen before.

You know how much I paid to those who administered justice in all those districts to which I came frequently. I think I distributed among them not less than the price of fifteen men, so that you might enjoy me, and I might always enjoy you in God. I am not sorry for it — indeed it is not enough for me; I still spend and shall spend more. God has power to grant

me afterwards that I myself may be spent for
your souls.

Indeed, I call God to witness upon my soul
that I lie not; neither, I hope, am I writing to you
in order to make this an occasion of flattery or
covetousness, nor because I look for honour
from any of you. Sufficient is the honour that is
not yet seen but is anticipated in the heart.
Faithful is He that promised; He never lieth.

But I see myself exalted even in the present
world beyond measure by the Lord, and I was
not worthy nor such that He should grant me
this. I know perfectly well, though not by my
own judgment, that poverty and misfortune
becomes me better than riches and pleasures.
For Christ the Lord, too, was poor for our
sakes; and I, unhappy wretch that I am, have no
wealth even if I wished for it. Daily I expect
murder, fraud, or captivity, or whatever it may
be; but I fear none of these things because of the
promises of heaven. I have cast myself into the
hands of God Almighty, who rules everywhere,
as the prophet says: *Cast thy thought upon God,
and He shall sustain thee.*

o, now I commend my soul to my faithful God, for whom I am an ambassador in all my wretchedness; but God accepteth no person, and chose me for this office — to be, although among His least, one of His ministers.

Hence let me render unto Him for all He has done to me. But what can I say or what can I promise to my Lord, as I can do nothing that He has not given me? May He search the hearts and reins; for greatly and exceedingly do I wish, and ready I was, that He should give me His chalice to drink, as He gave it also to the others who loved Him.

Wherefore may God never permit it to happen to me that I should lose His people which He purchased in the utmost parts of the world. I pray to God to give me perseverance and to deign that I be a faithful witness to Him to the end of my life for my God.

And if ever I have done any good for my God whom I love, I beg Him to grant me that I may shed my blood with those exiles and captives for His name, even though I should be denied a grave, or my body be woefully torn to pieces limb by limb by hounds or wild beasts, or the fowls of the air devour it. I am firmly convinced that if this should happen to me, I would have gained my soul together with my body, because on that day without doubt we shall rise in the brightness of the sun, that is, in the glory of Christ Jesus our Redeemer, as sons of the living God and joint heirs with Christ, to be made conformable to His image; for of Him, and by Him, and in Him we shall reign.

For this sun which we see rises daily for us because He commands so, but it will never reign, nor will its splendour last; what is more, those wretches who adore it will be miserably punished. Not so we, who believe in, and worship, the true sun — Christ — who will never perish, nor will he who doeth His will; but he will abide for ever as Christ abideth for ever, who reigns with God the Father Almighty and the Holy Spirit before time, and now, and in all eternity. Amen.

Behold, again and again would I set forth the words of my confession. I testify in truth and in joy of heart before God and His holy angels that

I never had any reason except the Gospel and its promises why I should ever return to the people from whom once before I barely escaped.

I pray those who believe and fear God, whosoever deigns to look at or receive this writing which Patrick, a sinner, unlearned, has composed in Ireland, that no one should ever say that it was my ignorance if I did or showed forth anything however small according to God's good pleasure; but let this be your conclusion and let it so be thought, that — as is the perfect truth — it was the gift of God. This is my confession before I die.

The *Lorica*
(Patrick's Breast-plate)

The beauty and lyricism of this most ancient of Irish hymns has long been admired and held in affection. A number of Irish prayers were known as Loricae, "breast-plates," the belief being that their incantation would protect those who recite them with a special power. Evidently this was a continuation of the older tradition of the pagan charm.

The oldest known copies of the present work date from a ninth century document but it is now generally held that the form and syntax of the language suggest a much more archaic origin.

The translation given here is substantially that of W. Stokes and J. Strachan, dating from 1903, with some later modifications by L. Bieler.

The preamble to the hymn itself, as found in the Irish Book of Hymns, *expresses the traditionally held view that Patrick and his companions were once saved from ambush by reciting the hymn and were turned into deer so as to be concealed from their enemies. For which reason the hymn is also known as "the Deer's Cry."*

 arise today
    through a mighty strength, the invoca-
      tion of the Trinity,
    through belief in the Threeness,
    through confession of the Oneness
    towards the Creator.

I arise today
    through the strength of Christ
      with His Baptism,
  though the strength of His Crucifixion
      with His Burial,
  through the strength of His Resurrection
      with His Ascension,
  through the strength of His descent
     for the Judgment of Doom.

I arise today
> through the strength of the love of
>> Cherubim,
> in obedience of Angels,
> in the service of the Archangels,
> in hope of resurrection to meet
>> with reward,
> in prayers of Patriarchs,
> in predictions of Prophets,
> in preachings of Apostles,
> in faiths of Confessors,
> in innocence of Holy Virgins,
> in deeds of righteous men.

I arise today
> through the strength of Heaven:
> light of Sun,
> brilliance of Moon,
> splendour of Fire,
> speed of Lightning,
> swiftness of Wind,
> depth of Sea,
> stability of Earth,
> firmness of Rock.

I arise today
 through God's strength to pilot me:
 God's might to uphold me,
 God's wisdom to guide me,
 God's eye to look before me,
 God's ear to hear me,
 God's word to speak for me,
 God's hand to guard me,
 God's way to lie before me,
 God's shield to protect me,
 God's host to secure me —
  against snares of devils,
  against temptations of vices,
  against inclinations of nature,
  against everyone who shall wish me ill,
  afar and anear,
  alone and in a crowd.

I summon today all these powers between me
      (and these evils) —
    against every cruel and merciless power
      that may oppose my body and my
      soul,
    against incantations of false prophets,
    against black laws of heathenry,
    against false laws of heretics,
    against craft of idolatry,
    against spells of women and smiths and
      wizards,
    against every knowledge that endangers
      man's body and soul.

Christ to protect me today
    against poison, against burning,
    against drowning, against wounding,
    so that there may come abundance of
        reward.
Christ with me, Christ before me, Christ
        behind me,
Christ in me, Christ beneath me, Christ
        above me,
Christ on my right, Christ on my left,
Christ where I lie, Christ where I sit, Christ
        where I arise,
Christ in the heart of every man who
        thinks of me,
Christ in the mouth of every man who
        speaks of me,
Christ in every eye that sees me,
Christ in every ear that hears me.

I arise today
> through a mighty strength, the invocation
>   of the Trinity,
> through belief in the Threeness,
> through confession of the Oneness
> towards the Creator.

Salvation is of the Lord.
Salvation is of the Lord.
Salvation is of Christ.
May Thy salvation, O Lord, be ever with us.

SAINT
PATRICK